FAITH

GRACE

(Three Levels of Faith)

DWAYNE NORMAN

Empyrion Publishing
Winter Garden FL 34787
info@EmpyrionPublishing.com

Grace, Faith, Rest

Copyright © 2016 by Dwayne Norman

ISBN: 978-1536873887

Empyrion Publishing
PO Box 784327
Winter Garden FL 34778
info@EmpyrionPublishing.com

Unless otherwise noted, all Scripture quotations are from the New King James Version of the Bible.

All rights reserved. No part of this book may be reproduced, stored in a retrieval system, or transmitted in any form or by any means – electronic, mechanical, photocopy, recording, or any other, without permission in writing from the author.

Printed in the United States of America

CONTENTS

1. The Attitude of Faith   5

2. The Law of Faith   43

3. The Rest of Faith   59

THE ATTITUDE OF FAITH

Chapter 1

It is so important that we understand how grace and faith work together resulting in supernatural rest for the Believer! While I was studying I Thessalonians 3:10 the Lord began to deal with me about my faith in Him.

"Night and day praying exceedingly that we may see your face and perfect what is lacking in your faith?"

The Apostle Paul prayed exceedingly night and day that God would use him to <u>perfect</u> what was lacking in their faith. As I thought about what he said to the Christians in Thessalonica I began to think about my faith. I wondered how much perfecting I needed to experience. Now the Lord Jesus is the only one who operated in perfect faith on this earth, but the rest of us are still growing and learning aren't we? I know that when we got saved the Lord gave each of us a measure of His faith (Romans 12:3). Jesus is the originator and developer of our faith (Hebrews 12:2). Even though we all got a measure of God's faith, we still must learn how to use it. Of course the "kind" of faith we have is the God-kind. Since our faith came from Him and He is God, then the only "kind" He would have, is the God-kind; therefore, we have the God-kind of faith.

The word "perfect" in the Greek in which this letter was written means to complete thoroughly, to repair or adjust. In the Amplified Bible it says it this way:

"[And we] continue to pray especially and with most intense earnestness night and day that we may see you face to face and mend and make good whatever may be imperfect and lacking in your faith."

Now think about this with me. If Christians cannot be lacking in their faith then why did the Holy Spirit lead Paul to pray earnestly that he would see their faces so he could perfect (complete, repair, mend and adjust) what was lacking in their faith? As I thought on that, I began to ask the Lord about my faith and did it need repairing, mending or adjusting? It is always good, no matter how long you have been in God's Word and walking with the Lord, and "convinced that all your doctrines are 100% correct", to continually examine your faith and what you believe <u>according to God's Holy Scriptures</u>; not according to your denominational statements of faith or how you were raised as a child.

The Attitude of Faith

Those things are fine as long as they agree and line up with the Word of God. If they do not line up with God's Word, then you need to make sure you stay on God's side even if your church asks you to leave and some of your relatives do not want to talk to you anymore. Of Course, whenever you are around these people continue sharing the Truth with them in love, but don't ever compromise your faith in God! Sometimes, I will pray and say, "Lord am I missing it anywhere in my life? Please show me. If I think that I have my act together and you know there are places in my life, attitudes, motives and what I believe that need to be corrected, tweaked and perfected in any way, please show me. I welcome you Holy Spirit to speak to me and change me everywhere I need it." After you say that prayer then allow Him to do it in your life. This is giving Him permission to perfect anything lacking in your faith.

Remember, the Holy Spirit and the Word of God always agree (I John 5:7)! If you say that the Spirit of God taught you something or gave you a revelation, it will always agree with chapter and verse from the Bible. If you have been walking with the Lord for 20, 30, 40 years don't let your pride hinder you from receiving correction. Please do not be one of those Christians (especially ministers) who say, "This is how I have always believed and I am not going to change it!" There are ministers who don't want to admit that some of their teaching is incorrect. They do not want to change their incorrect doctrines for fear of people leaving their church and or not esteeming them as spiritual as they originally thought of them.

Also, I do not think many ministries want to take the time (hours upon hours) to re-study how they have been trained to believe, so their teachings will line up with the Word of God. There are a lot of ministers who are comfortable in what they believe and they do not want anyone rocking the boat. There is nothing wrong with being comfortable in what you believe as long as it is Scripturally accurate. Listen! If God begins to show you an area in your understanding of the Word of God where you may be missing it, you need to have enough spiritual backbone and love for God's eternal Truth to change! Don't be stubborn and implacable! You could end up hurting yourself and those who listen to you. I heard a minister say that most Christians don't allow the Bible to get in the way of how they believe. Here is what Paul told Timothy, in I Timothy 4:16.

"Take heed to yourself and to the doctrine. Continue in them, for in doing this you will save both yourself and those who hear you."

Once again, if the Word of God is final authority and first place in your life and if it is what you live by then you need to humble yourself and admit that you have believed incorrectly on some things, and be willing to change. It may not always feel easy to allow the Holy Spirit to perfect what is lacking in our faith, but when we let Him do what is best for us then our faith in God will be strengthened and greatly increased!

Recently I was talking to a pastor on Facebook. I had mentioned that we need to use our faith to receive healing from God just like we received salvation.

The Attitude of Faith

He responded by saying, "Where does it say in the Bible that you need to use faith or operate in faith to receive healing?"

I was surprised when he asked that question because (in my opinion) it is really basic teaching or should be basic teaching for all Christians. What really bothered me was that this was a pastor of a church; a leader of the people in his congregation. If he did not understand the simplicity of faith in God for more than the new birth experience, then what spiritual level of understanding did his people have? On average, the spiritual knowledge and depth of understanding of the people in a church will not exceed that of their pastor; unless they are studying and hearing the Word through other ministers. Therefore, it is very important for us to pray for our pastors; that God will give them a spirit of wisdom and revelation in the knowledge of Christ and that the eyes of their understanding will be enlightened so they will comprehend and understand the mystery of Christ (Ephesians 1:17-19; 3:14-19).

For more teaching about the mystery of Christ and who you are in Him, please get our book "The Mystery" and "The Mystery Study Guide". Getting back to what this pastor wrote to me on Facebook, I got to thinking about what he said. Many times in the four Gospels, Jesus would tell people, "According to your faith be it unto you, be it unto you as you have believed and your faith has made you well." Jesus was the One who healed them but they had to operate in faith to activate His healing power to go into their bodies. In the King James Bible, Mark 11:24 says, **"Therefore I say unto you, What things soever ye desire, when ye pray, believe that ye receive them, and**

ye shall have them." Whatever you desire would include healing wouldn't it? God's Word says we have already been healed by Jesus' stripes (Isaiah 53:4, 5; Matthew 8:17; I Peter 2:24), but if you desire to experience it then you need to release your faith and receive it manifested in your body.

The same is true for salvation and all that Jesus finished for us at Calvary. The Lord doesn't want anyone to perish in hell, so He obtained salvation for every person, but to actually experience it, you must receive it by faith from His grace. If you choose not to receive, that does not nullify God's will for your salvation. He still wanted you to experience eternal life, but He will not make you receive. Let's look again at healing. God's Word is His will and His Word states that healing is available for everyone. If you choose not to receive it (for any reason), that does not nullify His will for your healing. He still wanted you to experience it whether you did or not. Just because you can give me some names of people in the Bible or out of the Bible who did not receive their healing does not change the fact that healing was still God's will for them. Even though they did not experience their healing, we are not going to throw away the Scriptures in the Bible that clearly state that healing was God's will for them. We may not know what happened in those people's lives, but the Word of God remains true and it will never change!! We should always side with God's Word and not anyone's experience, unless it agrees with Scripture! We do not judge the Word by people's experiences! We judge people's experiences by the Word! I pray that you will spiritually see and understand this and always examine everything you hear in the light of God's holy Word! Also, James 5:14, 15 says,

The Attitude of Faith

"Is anyone among you sick? Let him call for the elders of the church, and let them pray over him, anointing him with oil in the name of the Lord.

And the prayer of <u>faith</u> will save the sick, and the Lord will raise him up. And if he has committed sins, he will be forgiven."

Remember, the word "save" or salvation in the Greek is "Sozo" and it means to save, deliver, protect, <u>heal</u>, preserve, and <u>make whole</u>. Having faith for salvation means having faith to receive eternal life, deliverance, protection and healing; so faith isn't just necessary to be born again; it's necessary to receive anything from God's grace. I hope you can see how this minister I was talking to on Facebook needed some perfecting or adjusting concerning faith for healing. We all need to continually stay open for the Holy Spirit to change us, transform us and perfect anything lacking in our faith. I want to share something with you that I mentioned in my book "Just Believe" because it bears repeating.

A great teacher of faith was asked by a pastor why he taught on faith so much. He said according to Ephesians 2:8 we are <u>saved</u> by faith. No one can be saved or experience salvation without faith! He said according to Romans 1:17 the just shall <u>live</u> by faith. As Christians, we cannot live without faith! He said according to II Corinthians 5:7 we <u>walk</u> by faith. We cannot walk with God every day except by faith! Then he said according to II Thessalonians 1:3 our faith grows exceedingly or we <u>grow up</u> spiritually by faith. Also, he said according to Hebrews 11:6 we must operate in faith to <u>please God</u>. The Lord said that it is impossible to please Him without faith.

Therefore, we are saved, we walk, we live, we grow up and we please our Heavenly Father by **faith**! There are a lot of major subjects to study in the Bible, but I hope you can see that one of them is faith and it is extremely important!

In this book I want to share some things with you about three levels of faith. These three levels are like steps going up a staircase; you need to take one step at a time. If you try to go to level two and you are not established in your understanding of level one then it may seem like your faith is not working, causing you to be discouraged and give up. The same is true if you try to jump straight up to level three, skipping the first two levels. I believe that what you will learn in this book will greatly help you to understand that grace and faith depend on each other and work together. Grace needs faith and faith needs grace, and like I have already said, the result will be supernatural rest and great fruit produced in the Believer's life! The three levels we are going to look at are:
    1) The attitude of faith.
    2) The law of faith.
    3) The rest of faith.

Ephesians 4:23 says, **"And be renewed in the spirit of your mind."** Over the years we have had a lot of teaching on mind renewal according to Romans 12:2. It's true that we are transformed by the renewing of our minds to the Word of God. Having our minds renewed to God's Word is another one of those important subjects in the Bible. Yet, in Ephesians 4:23 the Apostle Paul said to be renewed in the <u>spirit</u> of our minds. What did he mean by that? How is that different than being renewed in our minds? What did he mean by the spirit of our minds? I believe that he is talking about our attitudes. Let me explain what I mean. Being renewed in the spirit of our minds is more than just memorizing a few more Scriptures; it is about the development of our spiritual attitudes. Now, please don't misunderstand me, our spiritual attitudes are connected to the renewal of our minds. The Amplified Bible says:

"And be constantly renewed in the spirit of your mind [having a fresh mental and spiritual attitude]."

"However, you were taught to have a new attitude." (God's Word Translation)

Let me share something very simple with you concerning what I mean about a renewed attitude. Galatians 3:13 says that Christ Jesus redeemed us from the curse of the law. We don't have room in this book to study this, but the curse of the law is everything that comes under the category of sin, sickness and poverty. When God redeemed us He bought us back to Himself; thus setting us free from what we were bound by. The cost was the priceless and precious Blood of Jesus through His death and resurrection! The word redeemed is in the past tense meaning that it has already been done; so I am not trying to get God to redeem me. The tense of the word "redeemed" as well as many other words in the New Covenant determines the kind of attitude we should have. Since sin, sickness and poverty are included in the curse of the law then I am redeemed (past tense) or free from all sin, sickness and poverty.

Grace, Faith, Rest

You and I as Believers are already free and delivered from the nature of sin and death, all of its consequences and from all of the sins we will ever commit (Romans 8:1, 2; Ephesians 1:7; Colossians 1:14); therefore, our attitude should never be, "I hope that God will forgive me of this". Also, it would not be Scripturally correct to say, "I am fasting and praying for God to forgive me, would it?" He already did that for us in Christ, through what Jesus <u>finished</u> for us at Calvary. Simply say, "Father, I receive the forgiveness that Jesus has already provided me through His Blood." We must recognize the efficacy and finality of all that Jesus suffered and accomplished for us through His entire substitutionary work. That is the correct attitude of faith. We need to have this kind of attitude about all that the Lord did for us. I know that many Christians will say they understand this but what they daily pray and confess contradict it. Maybe we need to get our Bibles out and go back and re-examine some of the things we believe?

If a lost person came to you and said that he was trying to quit smoking, chewing, cussing and was putting forth every effort to be a good person so that God would save him, you would probably correct him on the spot for his incorrect attitude. Granted, his attitude about desiring to demonstrate holiness is admiral, but it is also an attitude of works or self-effort; he's actually trying to earn his salvation isn't he? We know that salvation is a free gift from God by grace through faith (Ephesians 2:8), but we should also remember that everything else we receive from the Lord comes freely the same way.

If I came to you and said that I am fasting more, praying twice as much a day and feeding more poor people so God will heal me, you would again quickly correct me. You would remind me that like salvation I cannot earn my healing or anything from God. By the stripes of Jesus, I have already been healed. It is in the past tense and it's a done deal! Yet, many Christians who know this still conduct themselves in a way that contradicts what they claim to believe. Yes, we must have works of faith, but many Christians are replacing works of faith with self-effort or works of the flesh; while thinking they are operating in faith. So, when their healing isn't manifested, they become confused and discouraged. They don't understand why they are not healed, and they will say things like this, "I don't know why God hasn't healed me yet, because I am going to church more, praying more, fasting more and reading my Bible more…"

Can you hear their attitude? Their attitude is saying, "Lord, look at all of these good things I have done. Don't you see everything I have done for the church and your Kingdom? I have stepped out and made my move, now it is your turn to move!" They are trying to get God to respond to them, but operating in faith is about you and me responding to God. Let me say it like this, "All of our fasting, praying, reading and feeding the poor will not make our healing, prosperity, deliverance and redemption anymore "done and finished" than they already are! God moved once and for all at Calvary; it is now our move, but most of the Church is always praying for a "move" of God. That has been the problem. We have been waiting for God to "do something," and for the last 2000 years He has been waiting for His children to respond in faith to what He has already done.

We must get a revelation in our spirits that the Lord has already finished everything for us, and when we do, we will have a revelation of grace. The attitude of faith that I am referring to as the first level is actually an understanding and reality of the grace of God in our lives. Once again, if you have applied your faith for healing and after many months it has not come to pass, the devil will try to get you to consider other spiritual things you can do to get God to heal you. I emphasize "spiritual things" because they may be good spiritual disciplines, but if done with the wrong attitude they will actually be works of self-effort and not works of faith. As New Covenant Believers, we have never been under the Jewish laws; so, many times we don't relate to what Paul meant in Romans 6:14 about not being under the law but under grace.

When a Christian performs good and Godly works but from an attitude of self-effort and not from faith in Jesus' finished works, then, in many ways it is the same as operating under the law. So, for Believers, being free from the law means being free from an attitude of self-effort, an attitude of trying to get God to do something for us, hoping He will see our good works and show us favor. Ephesians 1:6 and John 17:23 say that we are already accepted in the Beloved and that God loves us as much as He loves Jesus; and that is true before you perform any good works for the Lord!! I Corinthians 13:2, 3 say:

"And though I have the gift of prophecy, and understand all mysteries and all knowledge, and though I have all faith, so that I could remove mountains, but have not love, I am nothing.

The Attitude of Faith

And though I bestow all my goods to feed the poor, and though I give my body to be burned, but have not love, it profits me nothing."

If you yield to the attitude that I must not be healed because I am not doing enough good things for the Lord, then you are putting yourself under the law and not under grace. Your good works may be helping other people but they will not profit you. You may say, "Well I don't care about profiting me. I just want to help others." When the Lord talks about profiting you, He is not talking about heaping things upon your lust. He is talking about learning how to use your faith to access God's grace (all the finished works of Christ); so you will not only have plenty of blessings for you and your family, but also plenty to give generously to others. If you don't correctly learn how to use your faith and receive from God, then you will dry up as a vessel for God use to spread the Gospel and to bless others!

As Christians, we are not under the Jewish laws because Jesus fulfilled those for us. We are now under grace (Romans 6:14), but when a Christian becomes performance minded, whether he realizes it or not, he is placing himself back under the law instead of under grace, and that will not work for a New Covenant Believer. If your thoughts are, "What do I need to do to get my healing or what do I need to do to get God's attention", then you are trying to live in the New Covenant by Old Covenant rules, and your faith will not work that way. You are trying to live by your good works instead of by faith in Jesus and His finished works. Jesus said to have faith in God (Mark 11:22). My faith is not in how much I go to church, or pray, or fast or feed the poor. My faith is not in my good works; now that doesn't stop me from having good works. I just don't put my faith in them. My faith is in the risen Christ Jesus and therefore in all that He finished for me at Calvary! Romans 1:17 says that the just shall live by faith. It did not say that the just shall live by good works. Remember again, our faith is not in how much we pray, fast and go to church. Our faith is in Jesus and in all that He accomplished for us through His entire substitutionary sacrifice.

When James 2:26 says that faith without works is dead, it's not talking about works of self-effort, but works of faith; there's a difference. For example, a work of faith is praising God that you are healed when you feel terrible. A work of self-effort is the result of not being 100% convinced that you are already healed and then coming up with something good to do for the Kingdom that you hope will get God's attention so He will do something about your healing. By doing this you are saying that you don't trust what God did for you in Christ and you are trying to get what you need on your own efforts.

I believe that many, many Christians are living with a performance attitude and don't even know it, because that is how they were taught. I have done the same thing many times in the past, but God has been perfecting my faith and teaching more about living by faith in His grace. By the way, did you know that you can believe and receive incorrect teaching from ministers who may love the Lord and be very sincere? They don't have to be ministers who are purposely trying to deceive Christians. These ministers can be lacking understanding in areas of God's Word and don't even realize it. The only one who has perfect knowledge about every subject in the Bible is Jesus, all the rest of us are still learning and growing. You may have listened over the years to preachers, who seemed to really love God, but a lot of their doctrines were not Biblical, and that is why you must study God's Word for yourself! No matter whom you are listening to, always examine what you hear in light of the Word of God. The same goes for my book you are reading, take time to look up all the Scriptures in your Bible and study them out for yourself.

The death and resurrection of Jesus is the foundation of Christianity. It separates the Old Covenant from the New Covenant. In our Bibles, we have God's Word in the Old and New Testaments, and we always will. God's Word will never change; it is the same both now and forever! We need to study the Word in our Bibles from Genesis to Revelation; while at the same time understanding that we are living in a New Covenant. The Old Covenant was great but Hebrews 8:13 says that it is now obsolete. God's Word in the Old Testament or Covenant is not obsolete, but the Old Covenant is. We have not lost anything by being under a New Covenant, but we have gained! Hebrews 8:6 says that this New Covenant is a better Covenant, which was established on better promises! Every good thing and every blessing in the Old Covenant plus much, much more is in the New Covenant!!

Now, here is where I believe the Lord has been directing us in our understanding. Faith in the New Covenant works the same way as faith worked in the Old Covenant, but the <u>attitude</u> of faith is different. II Corinthians 4:17 says:

"And since we have the same spirit of faith, according to what is written, "I believed and therefore I spoke," we also believe and therefore speak."

This is a good verse that shows a connection with faith in God in the Old Covenant and in the New Covenant. The Apostle Paul was quoting Psalm 116:10 in the Old Covenant and comparing it with faith in the New Covenant. The spirit of faith is the same in both Covenants. What is the spirit of faith? Paul said the spirit of faith refers to speaking words out of your mouth that you believe in your heart will come to pass, and that is exactly what Jesus said in Matthew 17:20; 21:21; Mark 11:23. The main way we release our faith to receive from God, is to say what we believe will come to pass. Therefore, Paul was telling us that this did not change after Jesus died and arose from the dead, but something did change, and it was our attitude of faith. The spirit of faith still works the same way but the attitude of faith is different.

Of course, we need to have a persistent and determined attitude of faith; an attitude that says I will not give up until my miracle comes to pass! But, the attitude that I am referring to is a different attitude than that. I am talking about an attitude that is inclusive to those in the New Covenant. I am talking about an attitude that came forth from Jesus' conquest of Satan, death, hell and the grave! It is an attitude of victory already accomplished! It is an attitude we can have because of the finished works of Christ! God's people did not have that privilege before the death and resurrection of Christ. This new attitude says, "I am not trying to get God to respond to me or to do anything for me because He has already done everything for me!!"

The Attitude of Faith

The new attitude of faith and declaration for every Christian is, "Everything is finished and completed for me in Christ and I already have the victory!" (Colossians 2:10; I John 5:4)

Before Jesus' death and resurrection no one could confess what was done for them in Christ because no one was in Him yet. No one could be born again before Calvary. No one could say the old man is dead and I am a new man in Christ. They were not redeemed from the curse of the law yet! They were not made God's righteousness in Christ yet! All of their sins had not been forgiven yet! They were not sons of God yet! The most they could be, were friends of God. A friend of God is wonderful, but friends are not heirs of God and joint heirs with Christ; only sons are! Think about that! We are in a much better covenant than they were in before Calvary!

In the Old Covenant, God would continually tell His people things they needed to do to get Him to move <u>in response to their actions</u>. In Deuteronomy 28:1, God told Israel that He would set them high above all nations **if** they obeyed His voice and observed all His commandments. He told them what they needed to do first to get Him to do something second, and in this case it was to seat them high above all the nations. As Christians, God has already seated us (in Christ) at His right hand in the Heavenly places (Ephesians 2:5, 6). It is already done! We are already seated there; whether or not we have obeyed any of the commandments. God is not waiting for me to obey His commandments so that He can seat me in the Heavenly places. He has already seated me there, and that is my place and position in Christ Jesus! Can you see that? God is not waiting for me to obey any commandments so that He can heal me or make me financially prosperous! Can you see that He has already finished everything for me at Calvary? So, where does obedience come in?

Obedience is still just as important now as it was then, but now I am not obeying God so that He will do something for me. I am not trying to find out what commandments or spiritual activities that I need to do so that God will bless me. In Christ, I am already blessed with the blessing of Abraham (Galatians 3:13-14, 29) and with all spiritual blessings in the Heavenly places (Ephesians 1:3)!! Listen closely; I am obeying Him in response to what He has already done for me (past tense) at Calvary. As a Believer, I am not trying to "move" God. He has already moved. I don't operate in faith and obey God's Word to move Him. Faith and obedience is how the Lord moves me to respond to and appropriate what He has already done.

Some Christians think that obedience to God's Word is not necessary anymore since Jesus finished everything for us at Calvary? Of course this is absolutely absurd, but if that is the way you think then you only have a revelation of grace and not of faith. If you only have a revelation of grace, then you will be a very passive Christian; one who thinks that all the finished works of Christ will just automatically come to pass. On the other hand, if all you have is a revelation of faith then you will probably be a very judgmental and legalistic Christian. We must have a revelation and understanding of grace and faith because they work together!

The Attitude of Faith

Ephesians 2:8 says for by <u>grace</u> you have been saved through <u>faith</u>. Romans 5:2 says through whom also we have access by <u>faith</u> into this <u>grace</u> in which we stand. Maybe this example will help. You could say that your checking account at the bank represents grace and your withdrawal slips represent faith. If you only have your checking account and no withdrawal slips, then you will not be able to get out or use any of your money; no matter how much is in your account. If you do not have a checking account but you have plenty of withdrawal slips, you still will not get any money. Can you see that you must have both of them: a checking account and withdrawal slips, they work together, not independent of each other?

Christians who believe that they have to do something first, to get God to do something for them, do not have a reality of all that Jesus did for them. If you really and truly believe in all the finished works of Christ, then you would know that there are not any commandments you can obey which will make the finished works of Christ more finished for you!! If they were done at Calvary, then they are done now; so let's start acting like it's true in our lives! Quit doing things (no matter how good they may be) with the attitude that you are trying to get God to respond to you. The New Covenant is not about the Lord responding to you and me; it's about you and me responding to His love for us and to everything Jesus finished for us at Calvary! Therefore, you cannot live under grace and enjoy all the blessings of Jesus' sacrifice while living under the law! If you read the Bible, you should know that grace and law (man's works of self-effort) don't mix.

Please let me reiterate this. Obedience to God's Word is very important! Obedience is faith in action, and it takes faith to access God's grace (Romans 5:2). Living under grace does not mean that everything the Lord did for us will just automatically appear in our lives. We still have to walk by faith and believe God just like they did in the Old Covenant; the only difference is, we are not releasing our faith and obeying God to try to get Him to do something for us. We are releasing our faith and obeying His commandments in response to what He has already done for us in Christ. This is how we experience the finished works of Christ in our daily lives. Can you see that we are talking about a change of attitude? You may be thinking that this is not a big deal, but I want you to know that it is a very huge and gigantic deal!

There is nothing wrong with doubling up on your reading, praying, fasting and giving to the poor; those are important things to do, but you need to be honest and ask yourself why you are doubling up on those things. Is it because your healing hasn't come to pass and you are hoping that God will see your great efforts (and be impressed by it) and manifest your healing? Are you trying to put pressure on God in the disguise of doing something spiritual and humanitarian? That way you can tell your Christian friends that after you started praying three hours a day instead of one hour, you got your healing. Can you hear the pride in that? In essence, you are saying that you finally figured out a way to get God to respond to you. You would be attributing the manifestation of your healing to your increased good works. I like what one minister said, **"God's response is not based on what I do, but on what Jesus did."**

The Attitude of Faith

Fasting is important, but don't go on a fast as a last ditch effort to impress the Lord, hoping that will motivate Him to manifest the money you need to pay your house payment; after which, you will probably tell your friends that the Lord led you on that fast. You and I both know if the money had come to pass sooner you would never have gone on the fast. Please understand that fasting is to change your heart towards God; not God's heart towards you. <u>Fasting is not an activity God has given us to put pressure on Him to answer our prayers!</u> Whenever you fast, do it with the attitude that you want to minister to the Lord, and you want to know Him better by spending the time in His Word and prayer that you would have normally spent eating a meal.

Many times we have no intention on fasting if the answer to our prayer comes to pass soon enough. Fasting is our final strategy on something that we think we can do to get God to move on our behalf. That is not grace! That is called works, and if you come to the Lord with your works of self-effort you will not receive from His grace, and if you cannot receive from His grace then you will not get anything! The only way to receive from God's grace is by faith! Romans 4:13, 14, 16 say:

"For the promise that he would be the heir of the world was not to Abraham or to his seed through the law, but through the righteousness of faith.
For if those who are of the law are heirs, faith is made void and the promise made of no effect,
Therefore, it is of faith that it might be according to grace, so that the promise might be sure to all the seed, not only to those who are of the law, but also to

those who are of the faith of Abraham, who is the father of us all."

God said that the only way to receive from Him is according to grace, and the only way to access His grace is through faith; not through works of self-effort. In Romans 11:6, the Spirit of God said:

"And if by grace, then it is no longer of works; otherwise grace is no longer grace. But if it is of works, it is no longer grace; otherwise work is no longer work."

The Lord will never lead us to perform works of self-effort; only works of faith which accesses His grace. Like I have already said, **most of the Church today is performance minded**. Most of the preaching is about what we need to do or quit doing to get God to "move" on our behalf, and that is not the correct attitude of faith for a New Covenant Believer. That is called works of self-effort or the law, and it will not work in the New Covenant! Yes, there are things we should do and things we should not do, but our obedience is not so that God will respond to us, but it's our way of responding to Him and receiving all that Jesus accomplished for us through His sufferings, death and resurrection.

Can you see how the devil has deceived and hoodwinked the Church through a lack of understanding about grace? A lot of the Church today is living as though under the law and not even aware of it. I believe this is one of the main reasons we have not received from God's grace. We thought that we were operating in faith but many times it was just our works of self-effort. We thought we were being spiritual; that is, we thought those good

The Attitude of Faith

works were necessary to get God to answer our prayers. When you really think about it, what we need to do as Christians to release our faith and access God's grace is to just say thank you to the Lord Jesus for all that He has done for us then expect it to be manifested in our lives. It is that simple!! And it should be that simple in our lives today! It was that simple when we got saved (when we received the greatest of all miracles) and it should be even easier for everything else we receive from God!

Again I heard a minister say, **"If God has not already provided what you need by grace, then your faith can't get it!"** The same is true for you and me as it was for the Apostle Paul, God's grace is sufficient! God's grace is more than enough for us! Everything we will ever need or desire is in the grace of God, it is time we learn how to make a withdrawal! When you pray, fast, go to church, help others and live a holy life because you love God and want to please Him, then you have a revelation of grace. If in your heart you are secretly hoping that the good things you are doing will "move" God to do something for you which He has already finished in Christ, then you are living as if you are under the law.

I am reminded of the story of Joseph when he was in Potiphar's house. Potiphar's wife tried to tempt him to commit adultery with her but Joseph refused. Do you remember what he said to her? He did not say, "I can't have a sexual relationship with you because I am believing God for a new chariot. I am trying to be holy in hopes that God will see my clean life and give me what I asked Him for." In Genesis 39:9 he said, **"There is no one greater in this house than I, nor has he kept back anything from**

me but you, because you are his wife. How then can I do this great wickedness, and sin against God?" In essence, Joseph said, "I am living a holy life, not because I am trying to get God to do something for me. I am living a holy life because I love God and I want to please Him." Let me ask you this question. Are you living a holy life because you think that God will not answer your prayers if you don't, or is it because you really love God and you know Him as your Heavenly Father and you only want to please Him?

We should be able to say, "The reason I serve God, walk in love towards others and live a holy life is because Jesus first loved me, suffered untold pain and torture for me, paid my penalty for sin, died and went to hell for me so I never have to go, arose from the dead, obtained eternal redemption and blessed me with all of the blessings of Heaven!!" My Heavenly Father has already given me every good thing in Christ; so I am not tithing, going to church and obeying His commandments to get Him to do something for me. I am doing all these things because I purpose in my heart to do them out of love for my Father God. I want to please Him. I don't want to ever sin against God! That is also called the fear of the Lord. This kind of attitude comes from a revelation of grace. Knowing that all my sins are forgiven past, present and future and I am washed clean by Jesus' precious Blood creates a desire in me to live a holy life! <u>A revelation of God's grace doesn't make me want to sin more</u>, but it makes me want to sin less. It creates an attitude in me like Joseph had, "I don't ever want to sin against God, but I always want to please and honor Him!" Titus 2: 11, 12 says:

The Attitude of Faith

"For the grace of God that brings salvation has appeared to all men,

Teaching us that, denying ungodliness and worldly lusts, we should live soberly, righteously, and godly in the present age."

A revelation of grace does not teach us to sin and live anyway we want to, thinking there are not any bad consequences to an ungodly lifestyle. Listen to the questions the Apostle Paul was asked in Romans 6:1, 2, 15.

"What shall we say then? Shall we continue in sin that grace may abound?

Certainly not! How shall we who died to sin live any longer in it?

What then? Shall we sin because we are not under law but under grace? Certainly not!"

Paul wrote this around 1900 years ago and he had to deal with some of the same questions we are asked today. Obviously, Paul was teaching on grace and some of the people were thinking that being under grace meant they could live any way they wanted to. If you read those verses again you will see that the Lord through Paul emphatically said "No!!!" to sin. He said being under grace does not mean you can live in sin!! Actually, it is just the opposite of that. As we just read in Titus Chapter two, when you truly understand the grace of God and how much He loves you, you will not have any desire to sin! If you truly love your Heavenly Father you will not want to do anything to displease Him! According to the Bible, a revelation of grace teaches me and creates in me a greater desire to live a holy life. The grace of God teaches me to deny ungodliness and worldly lusts and to live a righteous life in this present age! A revelation of God's grace gives me a greater understanding of how much God loves me! The more I comprehend and understand all that Jesus suffered for me to finish all that He finished for me makes me want to live and please Him more than ever! If you don't feel the same way to, you may want to reexamine your life to make sure you are really born again.

To be born again does not mean you will never sin again, it means that you now have power and dominion over sin (Romans 6:14). When you got saved, you became a new creation in Christ (II Corinthians 5:17, 18), but the "You" that became a new creation was just one-third of your entire person. You are made up of three parts: spirit, soul and body (I Thessalonians 5:23; Hebrews 4:12). The real "You" is your spirit; you possess a soul (mind, will and emotions) and live in a body. God is a spirit (John 4:24) and He created you in His image, therefore you are a spirit man (or woman). When you became a new creation in Christ, your spirit became brand new. The old nature of sin and death and all of the old things passed away and everything became new! That was only in your spirit though. Your mind (soul) and body did not become new. Your mind has to be renewed to the Word of God (Romans 12:2). You have to learn how to think like the new man, and that doesn't happen automatically.

Someone said, "How come I still want to sin after I have been born again?" If you are a new creation in Christ, your spirit man (the real you) does not want to sin, but your unrenewed mind still wants to tell your body to keep acting like the old man. Your unrenewed mind still thinks along the lines of living a sinful life, and it must be renewed! That is where discipleship comes in. You need to start studying and meditating in God's Word on all that Jesus did for you at Calvary and who you are in Him; until your mind starts thinking like the new man instead of like the old man (Ephesians 4:24; Colossians 3:8-10).

You have to learn how to live a holy life. You have to learn how to put on the new man. You don't automatically, 100%, start acting like the new man after you are born again! You will always be learning and growing for the rest of your life, but if you will learn to submit to the new nature in your spirit, yield every day to the Holy Spirit within and allow Him to have His way in your life, then He will change you on the outside. He will change you on the outside and help you to renew your mind and put on the new man, but He will do it from the inside out. I have several teaching books that will give you more understanding on this. Please visit our website at: www.dwaynenormanministries.org and get our books "The Mystery", "Defending the Faith" and "Are You Skilled in the Word of Righteousness". I also have audio teachings on these subjects as well as several messages called "Your identity in Christ" on youtube.com. Let's look at something the Lord Jesus said in Mark 11:25, 26:

And whenever you stand praying, if you have anything against anyone, forgive him, that your Father in heaven may also forgive you your trespasses.
But if you do not forgive, neither will your Father in heaven forgive your trespasses."

Now, I want to do a very quick review here. I need to make sure we are on the same page of understanding when we talk about the time that Jesus walked this earth and what that meant. Our Lord walked this earth and ministered to the people while in the Old Covenant. Even though the four Gospels are in the New Testament, they contain the teachings of Christ that were given to us while He was living in the Old Covenant. The death and resurrection of Christ separated the Old Covenant from the New Covenant. Before Calvary, no one could be born again. No one could have their sins washed away and receive a new and clean conscience by the Blood of Jesus (Hebrews 10:1-4). God's people were still under the Jewish laws when Jesus arrived on the scene and He came to fulfill those laws. So, as we have discussed, before Calvary, everything was about what man needed to do to get God to do something for man.

In these two verses that we just read, the Lord said that God would not forgive us if we don't forgive others. In other words, we have to do something first to get God to do something second. In this case, we have to forgive first so that God will forgive us. Now let me remind you of some verses in the New Covenant.

"And every priest stands ministering daily and offering repeatedly the same sacrifices, which can never take away sins.
But this Man, after He had offered one sacrifice for sins forever, sat down at the right hand of God.
This is the covenant that I will make with them after those days, says the Lord: I will put My laws into their hearts, and in their minds I will write them,"

Then He adds, "Their sins and their lawless deeds I will remember no more." (Hebrews 10:11, 12, 16, 17)

The phrase "After those days" is referring to after the death and resurrection of Jesus. The covenant that God has made with us is talking about this New Covenant, and in this Covenant all of our sins and lawless deeds have been washed away by Jesus' precious Blood! We have touched on this some already, but I want to bring out a few more things. What we need to understand is that all of our sins past, present and future are forgiven! Let me remind you of some verses in the Bible.

"And from Jesus Christ, the faithful witness, the firstborn from the dead, and the ruler over the kings of the earth. To Him who loved us and washed us from our sins in His own blood,
And has made us kings and priests to His God and Father, to Him be glory and dominion forever and ever. Amen." (Revelation 1:5, 6)

"In Him we have redemption through His blood, the forgiveness of sins, according to the riches of His grace." (Ephesians 1:7)

"In whom we have redemption through His blood, the forgiveness of sins." (Colossians 1:14)

"Who being the brightness of His glory and the express image of His person, and upholding all things by the word of His power, when He had by Himself purged our sins, sat down at the right hand of the Majesty on high." (Hebrews 1:3)

Grace, Faith, Rest

Through Jesus' one sacrifice He has forgiven and washed all of our sins away forever! When Jesus ascended into Heaven and sat down that was confirmation that He finished everything He came to do. He purged us of our sins once and forever! Now, that does not mean that a Christian cannot sin. It means that we are free from the power and dominion of sin (Romans 6:2, 11, 14-15)! It means that if you do sin, you can receive forgiveness for that sin. What we need to understand is that Jesus does not have to go back and die for our sins every time we commit a sin. He has paid the price for us once and for all; therefore, He has already forgiven us of all of the sins we will ever commit. You may not have thought about this before, but Jesus (through His Blood) has forgiven you of all of the sins you have not yet committed.

You may say, "I believe that Jesus finished everything for me at Calvary!" My question is, "Are you sure that you really believe that?" If we commit a sin, Jesus does not have to shed His Blood again for us does He? Forgiveness is already available for us; since it is already done for us then why would we need to actually ask God *if* He would forgive us for something that He has already forgiven us of? According to I John 1:9 (which was written to Christians, not to unbelievers), if you commit a sin of any kind then confess it to the Lord and simple receive your forgiveness. If I said or did something that displeased the Lord, I would probably say, "Father, your Word says that Jesus forgave and washed away all of my sins forever; therefore, I receive forgiveness for this sin, and I thank you Father for forgiving me."

The Attitude of Faith

The same is true for healing, prosperity and everything Jesus blessed us with through Calvary. By Jesus' stripes I was healed almost 2000 years ago; therefore, I am healed right now, no matter how my body looks or feels. So, I don't need to ask the Lord if He will heal me because He already has; I just need to say something to the effect, "Lord, I release my faith to appropriate what you have already done for me. I simply receive my healing for my body right now in Jesus' Name!" From that point on, I call my body healed, whole and strong! I declare that I am living in perfect health every day in Jesus' Name! I rejoice and give God all the glory for it, as if it were already manifested! That is how you put works with your faith and that is how you release your faith to access God's grace.

All that I have said in the last few pages, was to explain what I wanted to say about Mark 11:25, 26. I hope you can see now that when Jesus said that God won't forgive you if you don't forgive others would only apply to people living before Calvary, or before Jesus forgave and washed away all of our sins past, present and future. Please understand this, we still must forgive others. We cannot harbor unforgiveness in our hearts because that can open up a door in your life for the devil to come in and cause you problems. It can open up a door for sickness and disease to come in. We need to always be quick to forgive, slow to speak and slow to wrath, but it is not so that God will forgive us; because He already has. That is why I asked you the question, "Are you really sure you believe that Jesus cleansed you of all your sins through His precious Blood?"

When I got divorced in 1993, my first thought was that I am going to have to forgive my ex-wife or God will not forgive me (based on Mark 11:25, 26). Even though I had no desire in my heart to forgive her, I still believed (by the way I was taught) that if I did not forgive her then God would not forgive me. Obviously, I did not have a revelation of grace then like I do now. So, the devil tried to take advantage of my ignorance. If you had asked me if I believed that Jesus washed away all of my sins, I would have quickly said yes, but I still did not "put two and two together". I did not understand that because of what Jesus finished for me through His atonement; God was not waiting for me to forgive my ex-wife before He could forgive me. Still, I needed to forgive her so that I would not give the devil any place in my life. God has already forgiven you and me of all of our sins and of every sin we will ever commit. This is clearly revealed to us in the Scriptures in the New Covenant; either God's Word is true or it's not. I believe in all the finished works of Christ, don't you? Think of all the Christians that have ignorantly suffered guilt and condemnation from the hand of the devil because they thought God would not forgive them until they forgave someone.

I struggled for a couple of years thinking that God would not forgive me of my sins because I had not forgiven my ex-wife. God knew my heart and He knew that I could not honestly forgive her from my heart within just a couple of days. It took about two years for the Holy Spirit to change my heart so that I could truly say that I have forgiven her, but during that time I kept thinking that God would not forgive me. I kept thinking about what Jesus said in Mark 11:25, 26. I did not realize that what He said

The Attitude of Faith

only applied to those people who lived before Jesus died and arose from the dead; because their sins had not yet been cleansed by Jesus' Blood.

Think of the peace I could have experienced during those two years if I really understood that through Jesus' death and resurrection all my sins were washed away forever! I did not fully understand that all of my sins past, present and future were already forgiven. I thought I understood that back then, but now I realize that I was lacking revelation about God's grace that would have helped me tremendously had I known it. Please let me reiterate. God is not waiting for you to forgive someone before He will forgive you, but you still need to forgive that person. Unforgiveness is one of the devil's main deceptive ways to get a foothold in the lives of Christians; so I strongly encourage you to please keep that door closed (locked shut!) by always being quick to forgive; even if it was the other person's fault! No matter who's fault it was, forgive the other person as well as yourself in Jesus' Name and you will keep that door closed off to the devil! God is love! Always walk in love and you will always walk in God!

Since no one could be saved before Jesus died and arose from the dead then how did Jesus respond to someone who wanted to have eternal life? Mark 10:17, 19 say:

"Now as He was going out on the road, one came running, knelt before Him, and asked Him, "Good Teacher, what shall I do that I may inherit eternal life?"

"You know the commandments: 'Do not commit adultery,' 'Do not murder,' 'Do not steal,' 'Do not bear false witness,' 'Do not defraud,' 'Honor your father and mother.'"

It is very clear in this verse that this man wanted to know how to be saved or have eternal life. Did Jesus tell him to pray the "Sinners prayer or prayer of salvation" with Him? No He didn't. He started talking to him about the commandments, didn't He? Why? Man was still under the law at the time when Jesus walked this earth. The Lord was telling him that all he could do at that time was to obey God's laws and commandments. Yes, he could believe in what Jesus was about to do at Calvary, but he still could not experience having his sins washed away by the Blood of Jesus and being born again. Now, let's look at an example that took place after the death and resurrection of Jesus. Acts 16:27-31 say:

"And the keeper of the prison, awaking from sleep and seeing the prison doors open, supposing the prisoners had fled, drew his sword and was about to kill himself.
But Paul called with a loud voice, saying, "Do yourself no harm, for we are all here."
Then he called for a light, ran in, and fell down trembling before Paul, and Silas.
And he brought them out and said, "Sirs, what must I do to be saved?"
So they said, "Believe on the Lord Jesus Christ, and you will be saved, you and your household."

The Attitude of Faith

Notice, the man asked Paul basically the same question as the other man asked Jesus, but Paul gave him a totally different answer didn't he? Why didn't Paul give the man a list of commandments to obey? The answer of course is because they were not under the law anymore, but under grace. Jesus had already died and arose from the dead. Paul simple told him that all he needed to do now to have eternal life is to <u>believe</u> on the Lord Jesus Christ, and that is what Paul wrote in Romans 10:9.

"That if you confess with your mouth the Lord Jesus and believe in your heart that God raised Him from the dead, you will be saved."

All of God's Word is true in the Old and New Testaments, but not everything God told Israel while under the law applies to us today, and you will get yourself into trouble if you bring things that were only for people under the law and try to make them apply to people under grace. For example, tithing is very important and all Christians should be faithful and cheerful tithers and givers. Tithing was in operation before the law was given through Moses, during the time of law and is still now true for all Believers under grace in this New Covenant! But, the attitude about the tithe was different for those under the law when compared to the attitude Christians should have about the tithe now that we are under grace (For more teaching on the tithe please get our book "The Prosperous Seed" through our website: www.dwaynenormanministries.org).

Under the law, in Malachi Chapter three, God's people were commanded to tithe and give offerings. If they did not do it a curse would come on them, but if they did

Grace, Faith, Rest

do it then God would bless them and rebuke the devour. After Calvary, under grace, God has told us in His Word (II Corinthians 9:7; Ephesians 1:3; 4:7) to give because we purpose in our hearts to give. We don't tithe and give because we have to. We don't tithe to try to get God to bless us; we are already blessed with every spiritual blessing in Christ! Tithing is one of the ways we release our faith to appropriate what the Lord has already given us.

A farmer doesn't have to sow any seed in the ground. There is no law that says he must sow seed, but if he chooses not to sow anything (and he can make that choice if he wants to), he will not reap anything. There are natural laws and spiritual laws that God set into motion (Genesis 8:22; II Corinthians 9:6-8) a long time ago. These laws of sowing and reaping worked before the law was given through Moses, they worked during the time of the law and they work today for us living under grace. Once again, you don't have to tithe and give, but if you want to experience all of the good things Jesus blessed you with through Calvary then you must release your faith to access God's grace (Romans 5:2). One of the main ways to release your faith to experience the blessings that are already yours in Christ is to cheerfully tithe and give into the work of the Lord.

Also, we don't tithe so that God will rebuke the devil (devour) for us. He has already given us all authority and power over the devil and told us to resist him and he will flee from us (James 4:7)! Jesus conquered the devil for us at Calvary and gave us the victory! **You speak to the devil, sickness, poverty and whatever he is bringing**

against you and command it to leave in Jesus' Name and they have to obey you!!

One more thing, a curse will not come on you if you don't tithe. Christ (through His death and resurrection) has already redeemed us from the curse of the law (Galatians 3:13, 14)! Since we are redeemed (free) from the curse of the law, we are totally free from all curses of any kind; which would include any "Generational curses"!! You don't have to try to figure out what generational curses were in your family tree! You are free and redeemed by Jesus' shed Blood from anything that may have been there!! So, don't let the devil get you into fear about any kind of sicknesses or diseases! You are free from them all, but still let me remind you of some things that we are redeemed from that were under the curse.

"Moreover He will bring back on you all the diseases of Egypt, of which you were afraid, and they shall cling to you,
Also every sickness and every plague, which is not written in this Book of the Law, will the Lord bring upon you until you are destroyed.
Your life shall hang in doubt before you; you shall fear day and night, and have no assurance of life,
In the morning you shall say, 'Oh, that it were evening!' And at evening you shall say, 'Oh, that it were morning!' Because of the fear which terrifies your heart, and because of the sight which your eyes see." (Deuteronomy 28:60, 61, 66, 67)

I hope that sometime you will read (Deuteronomy 28:1-14) about all the blessings that are yours in Christ since you are now Abraham's seed (Galatians 3:7, 9, 29).

Grace, Faith, Rest

Now, don't stop at Deuteronomy 28:14 though, continue reading Chapter 28: 15-68, and you will learn about all the curses that you are free and redeemed from! You are free from all fears! We should never be afraid of the devil or anything we have been redeemed from!! Also, you will learn about all the evil things that you do not have to put up with in your life and how you can live totally free from them!! You are under grace now and God's grace is more than enough! Through the grace of God, you have all sufficiency in all things and are complete in Christ Jesus (II Corinthians 9:6-11; Colossians 2:3, 10)!! Expect to live your life everyday absolutely free from all curses, and blessed with all the blessings of Heaven!! Remember, release your faith and expect everything Jesus finished for you and blessed you with through His substitutionary sacrifice to be manifested in every area of your life!! Expect to see it, feel it and experience it in Jesus' Name because it all belongs to you!! God loves you so much and all His goodness and grace are yours!!

THE LAW OF FAITH

Chapter 2

I am so glad to know that when we got saved, God imparted into our spirits a measure (or as the King James Bible says in Romans 12:3 …the measure of faith). The Lord Jesus is the author (originator) and developer of our faith (Hebrews 12:2). Every Christian has faith to walk by, yes, faith to live by. So, don't ever listen to the devil if he tells you that you don't have any faith! As Christians, we have a measure of God's world creating, mountain moving faith and we need to learn how to use it. Remember, Jesus said that all things are possible to him who believes (Mark 9:23)! If you are a Believer, then all things are possible for you freely from God's grace through faith in Jesus! Now, that is great news!!

"Therefore by the deeds of the law no flesh will be justified in His sight, for by the law is the knowledge of sin. (Romans 3:20)

Do we understand what the Lord meant when He said by the deeds of the Law? For you and me today (in the New Covenant) it would be like saying by the deeds of self-effort or works of the flesh (doing things to get God's attention or trying to earn something from Him). We can't be justified and we can't be healed, blessed, delivered or set free by our good works; only by and through the grace of God.

"But now the righteousness of God apart from the law is revealed, being witnessed by the Law and the Prophets,
even the righteousness of God through faith in Jesus Christ, to all and on all who believe. For there is no difference." (Romans 3:21, 22)

I know that you probably already know this, but the reason we are God's righteousness in Christ (II Corinthians 5:21) is because of our faith in Jesus. The Law and the Prophets in the Old Testament witnessed to this but could not make it happen. All of our good works could not give us a new spiritual nature (eternal life) and make us righteous; Jesus freely accomplished that for us at Calvary.

"Where is boasting then? It is excluded. By what law? Of works? No, but by the law of faith.
Therefore, we conclude that a man is justified by faith apart from the deeds of the law.

The Law of Faith

Or is He the God of the Jews only? Is He not also the God of the Gentiles? Yes, of the Gentiles also,

since there is one God who will justify the circumcised by faith and the uncircumcised through faith.

Do we then make void the law through faith? Certainly not! On the contrary, we establish the law." (Romans 3:27-31)

The Apostle Paul said that our personal works of self-effort had absolutely nothing to do in making us righteous in Christ; therefore, what do we have to boast about? The answer is nothing, but I like the way he said it in verse 27. He said by what law? In other words, did we set some kind of law in motion so that we could experience God's righteousness? The answer is yes, but what law? Was it works or you could say the law of works? No, but it was a law though and Paul called it the law of faith. Did you know that faith is a law?

If someone deposited one million dollars in my bank account and told me that I can get out as much as I want, any time that I want, I would not have anything to boast about would I? I would have a lot of money in my account even though I personally did not put it in there. That money would not be there because of my good works would it? I had nothing to do with it. What I should do is say thank you to the person who made the deposit and start enjoying my financial blessing. That's what the Body of Christ needs to do today! Let's say thank you to Jesus for all that he finished for us and blessed us with at Calvary. You could say that He put every good thing that He has into our

Heavenly, grace account, and the way to make a withdrawal is with our faith.

Let me remind you that the natural and the spiritual realms operate according to laws and forces. Why do we use the term natural law and spiritual law? What is a law? A dictionary meaning of the word "law" is:

A formulation describing a relationship that is presumed to hold between or among phenomena for all cases in which the specified conditions are met.

Please don't let that definition confuse you. All it is saying is that a law is something that always works unless another condition is introduced that can override the law. The reason we call gravity a law is because every time you throw something into the air it always (without fail) comes down. Even when an airplane lifts off the ground and starts flying, it seems like the law of gravity is not working, but it is. The reason a plane can seem to defy gravity is because other laws and forces (conditions) have been introduced to override the law of gravity, but they still did not eliminate the law of gravity did they? When the laws of lift and thrust are applied, the airplane will take flight, but if you turn the engine off it will descend quickly; proving that the law of gravity never stopped working.

Now, if someone (living of course on this earth) comes to you saying that the law of gravity does not work, would you believe him? No, not if you have any sense. You would try to nicely tell him that he is wrong and obviously has missed it somewhere. He might have been in a situation or saw something that appeared to him like the law of gravity wasn't working, but we still know that it was working don't we? Even though he does not understand what happened, his ignorance does not negate the law of gravity. God's Word is God's will for man. You could say that the Word of God is spiritual law. That means it always works! If you don't think it does, then you are wrong, you have missed it somewhere. God's Word teaches us that salvation, healing, deliverance and prosperity are His will for every Believer. God's will, as revealed in the Bible is established forever for us; like the law of gravity it always works, but it is also much greater than the law of gravity. The law of gravity can be superseded by higher laws and forces, but God's Word (His spiritual law) cannot! There is nothing higher or more powerful than the Word of God!

So, if you are trusting the Lord for the manifestation of a healing or financial miracle and it has not come to pass, don't dare say, "I guess it's not God's will for me to be healed and prosperous." Even though you do not understand why your miracle is not manifested does not mean that it is not God's will for you to have it. In other words, your spiritual ignorance will not negate God's will for you. It can cause you not to experience God's will for your life, but if you don't experience, for example, your healing, it does not mean that God's will was not healing for you. The reason faith is called a law is because it always works when you set it in motion. The law of faith always works; whether you allow it to work in your life or not. Through lack of knowledge and understanding you can keep the law of faith from working <u>for you</u>, but you cannot stop the law of faith itself from being a spiritual law that always works. I hope that you can understand this.

Grace, Faith, Rest

If you feel that you have released your faith for the manifestation of your healing and it seems that after a long period of time it hasn't come to pass, don't assume that the law of faith doesn't work. That would be like assuming that the law of gravity doesn't work. You need to stop and realize that you must be missing it somewhere or there is something you don't understand. Faith in God always works! I like the fact that God describes faith as the law of faith because that guarantees me that my faith will always work for me when I learn how to release it. Since gravity is considered a law, I never doubt that it will work, and gravity is just a natural law. How much more confidence I should have in the law of faith! The law of faith is a spiritual law of God's Kingdom and it cannot fail! The devil does not have any spiritual or natural laws that can override God's spiritual laws.

When Jesus prayed for Peter's faith not to fail, He was praying that Peter would maintain his faith in God, and he did; whereas Judas quit operating in faith and gave up. Luke 22:32 in the Message Bible says:

"Simon, I've prayed for you in particular that you not give in or give out…" The Easy to Read Bible says:

"I have prayed that you will not lose your faith…!"

So, I hope you can see that we can turn the law of faith on or off in our lives, it's up to us; but the law of faith always works. Now, here is the question we should ask ourselves, "Are we really sure that we are in faith?" That gets back to the Scripture I started with in the first chapter about our faith being perfected. We need to put our faith

The Law of Faith

in the integrity of God's Word and in His faithfulness to honor it in our lives rather than in our good works. Good works are very important but they should be the fruit of our faith in God, not the root. In Mark 11:22, Jesus said to have faith in God. Therefore, my faith is not in how much I pray, read the Bible, fast and give to the poor. My faith is in a person, the Lord Jesus Christ and in all of His finished works. Do you see that?

Here is how you can test your attitude to see if it is of faith or of works. Let's say that you hear about a Christian being healed of a terrible disease, and as far as you know that person never prays, studies the Bible or goes to church. If your first thought is, "I don't understand why he got his healing and mine has not come to pass yet. I pray 2 hours a day, read 5 chapters out of my Bible a day, go to church 3 times a week and volunteer 1 day a week to take blankets and food to the homeless." Those are wonderful things you are doing but if that is your first thought when you hear about how God blessed someone else then you are self-centered and you don't have a revelation of grace. You are still living under "law" or works of self-effort and not by faith in Jesus and His finished works. You thought you were in faith by all the good, spiritual things you have been doing but your thoughts and motives prove differently. You thought that the Lord would surely manifest your healing because of all the good and humanitarian works you've done.

Many Christians go all of their lives thinking this way and assuming they are operating in strong faith while seeing no results, and they are clueless to their problem. They think because God sees all their good works that everything is fine and they are not missing it in any are of their lives. They think their good and spiritual works for the Kingdom of God cover up their true motives and attitudes. Yes, we should have lots of good works but they should be the fruit born out of our intimate walk with the Lord and our believing that everything has already been done for us in Him. Our good works should come forth from a heart that loves and wants to please God, not from a heart that just wants to get His attention in hopes that we can convince Him to bless us. Let's don't secretly do good things to help others out of motives of selfishness to be seen by men or by God, but out of motives of love for God and people.

In chapter one, we talked about the spirit of faith and how it is the same in the Old and New Covenants. The Holy Spirit through Jesus and Paul told us the main way to release our faith. We must speak words out of our mouths that we believe in our hearts will come to pass; that is how to set the law of faith in motion, and once it is set in motion it will always work. You and I can set the law of faith in motion in our lives any time we want to, and we can also turn it off. I am convinced that probably all of us many times in our lives have turned the law of faith off and did not even realize it. We turned it off because our miracle, healing, financial blessing, etc. did not come to pass fast enough. The question is how did we do that? We have already talked about one of the answers to this but I want to look at it from Romans 4:13, 14.

"For the promise that he would be the heir of the world was not to Abraham or to his seed through the law, but through the righteousness of faith.

The Law of Faith

For if those who are of the law are heirs, faith is made void and the promise made of no effect."

In verse 14, when Paul says that if those who are of the law are heirs then faith is made void, he is telling us that one of the main ways we have turned off the law of faith in our lives. In these verses, when he talks about the law he is contrasting works with faith. Many times we have set the law of faith into operation in our lives but when our miracle or healing did not come to pass fast enough we tried to come up with a new idea on "how to get God to manifest our miracle", and remember, any other way besides faith in God's grace will not work! We decided to double up on our praying, studying and fasting hoping God will see that and do something for us, but without realizing it we voided out our faith. We did not stop the law of faith from working; we just stopped it from working in our lives. By increasing our good works while operating in a wrong attitude we actually substituted our good works for faith. Paul was telling the Christians in Rome that if they continued to operate under the law then they were substituting the law for faith; thus voiding out their faith. When they made their faith void they made the promise of no effect. That means they did not experience the blessings God had for them. The same is true for us today. We cannot experience and enjoy God's blessings in our lives except freely from God's grace through faith in Jesus and all that He finished for us!

Do you realize how important the grace of God is? When I was a young man growing up in Florida, I was raised in a Southern Baptist Church and if you asked anyone in the church what grace was, they would always say the unmerited favor of God, and that is very correct. Grace is God showing us favor when we did not deserve it, but being a teenager who read about the miracles of Jesus, I wanted to see a demonstration of God's power, and it seemed to me like grace had nothing to do with the power of God. That was around 40 years ago and I now have a better understanding of grace. I know now that grace is actually the operation of God's power in our lives because of the favor He shows us through Jesus' death and resurrection. Grace is God's riches at Christ' expense. John 1:17 said that the law came through Moses but grace and truth came through Jesus. Everything Jesus finished for us and blessed us with is in the grace of God. All salvation, healing, deliverance, prosperity, protection, peace, wisdom and all the blessings of Heaven are included in God's grace. One day while I was reading Hebrews 2:9 God gave me a greater revelation of grace.

"But we see Jesus, who was made a little lower than the angels, for the suffering of death crowned with glory and honor, that He, by the grace of God, might taste death for everyone."

When I read the part that says, "…He, by the grace of God…" the Holy Spirit really drew my attention to that. For some reason I never thought about Jesus needing God's grace to redeem us. I guess it was because I knew that Jesus was sinless so why would He really need any grace? He was morally perfect. I grew up thinking that because we were not sinless and perfect, we would need a lot of grace, or we would need for God to show us a lot of favor; but why would Jesus need grace? I think a lot of Christians only relate grace to forgiveness of sin. If that is the only understanding you have of grace, then you would not understand why Jesus needed grace; because He never sinned.

As I meditated on this I began to see that Jesus did not need grace because He had sinned, but for the operation of God's power in His life to enable Him to accomplish all that He did. Again, grace gives us more than just the forgiveness of sins. All of the strength, wisdom, endurance, love and compassion the Lord needed to suffer all that He suffered before going to the cross; as well as from the cross to the throne was in the grace of God! What really hit home with me was, if my Lord and Savior needed the grace of God, how much more did I! Praise God for His awesome grace!! I'm so glad I am under grace, living in a New Covenant of grace and have an abundance of grace in my life!! It is all because you and I are in Christ! All the forgiveness, peace, wisdom, healing and financial prosperity that you need are in the grace of God. Here is what the Lord told us in II Corinthians 9:8.

"And God is able to make all grace abound toward you, that you, always having all sufficiency in all things, may have an abundance for every good work."

Wow, through the grace of God we have all sufficiency in all things; that sounds like abundant life and more than you will ever need or desire for every area of your life!! Well, does that mean that it will automatically come to pass in our lives now, since we are living under grace? The Apostle Paul gave us some explanation about that in Romans 5:1, 2.

"Therefore, having been justified by faith, we have peace with God through our Lord Jesus Christ,

Through whom also we have access by faith into this grace in which we stand, and rejoice in hope of the glory of God."

In verse two, he said that through Jesus (where all grace and truth originate) we have <u>access</u> into this grace in which we stand. So, because we are in Christ, we are now <u>standing</u> every day in God's grace! Romans 5:17 says that through Jesus Christ we have received an <u>abundance</u> of grace! Also, Ephesians 4:7 says that to each one of us grace was <u>given</u> according to the measure of Christ's gift! Therefore, as Christians, we have been given the grace of God, we are standing in the grace of God and we have an abundance of the grace of God! We should greatly rejoice in that Truth, but Romans 5:2 said that we still have to access that grace. That clearly means that all the riches of the inheritance that belongs to us in Christ will not automatically be manifested in our lives. The Lord said it must be accessed or another way to say it is, we need to learn how to make withdrawals out of our Heavenly "bank account" or our Heavenly grace account.

My wife and I have a checking account at the bank and we have some money in it. Even though there is money in our account, it doesn't automatically appear in my wallet. I still have to access my checking account if I want to experience and enjoy what is already mine. I hope that you are seeing this! The money in my account belongs to me, so I don't have to pray and fast for God or the banker to put some money in my account, but I still <u>have to</u> make a withdrawal! The Lord told us in Romans 5:2 exactly how

The Law of Faith

to make a withdrawal. He said that we have access <u>by faith</u> into this grace. At the bank, you must use a withdrawal slip to access your account, and you know it works every time. When it comes to our grace account, the withdrawal slip is the measure of faith God gave us when we got saved. You could say that God opened up an account for you and me in our names, put unlimited blessings in it and then gave us what we needed to make all the withdrawals we will ever need! Praise God for His goodness in our lives!!

Now, what if I go to my banker and tell him that I have doubled up on my praying, reading the Bible, fasting and giving to the poor, so he should give me whatever amount of money I desire from my checking account? Will he then give me whatever I want, even though the money is in my account? No he won't! He may say, "Those are a lot of nice things you are doing to please the Lord and help others but you still have to make a withdrawal if you want to get any money out of your account."

Let me give you another scenario. What would you say to a fellow Believer who has $200,000.00 in his bank account, the mortgage company is foreclosing on the $100,000.00 debt owed on his house, and he says, "I just don't understand why God is allowing this to happen to me? I am a Deacon in my church. I am on the board. I am the one who financed the youth mission trip and I am also the one who raised all the money to give presents to 100 children last Christmas. I just don't know why this is happening to me. I thought God loves me. I know I am not perfect, but I try to do my best to help others?" I know that you might want to slap some sense into him but you have to walk in love. You would probably ask him why he has not made a withdrawal out of his bank account and paid off the debt wouldn't you? I would dare say that most people with any common sense would never do that in the natural realm. Christians and non-Christians know that quoting your good works to the banker is not how you get money out of your account; you still must make a withdrawal or you will not be able to actually use the money that belongs to you.

Most people know that if the money is in their account all they have to do is make a withdrawal and pay the mortgage off, but how come many Christians can't seem to figure that out when it comes to making a spiritual withdrawal from God's grace? They will automatically start telling God about all of the good works they have done for His glory, how many people they have sacrificed their time to help, while hoping (secretly in their hearts) that God is impressed and will respond to their works of self-effort, but He will not respond to that. Remember, we are not waiting on God to do any responding, He is waiting on us! We have to respond to grace. Faith accesses God's grace. When you believe in all that Jesus finished for you at Calvary and start declaring it done in your life, you are then releasing your faith (making a withdrawal) to access God's grace.

For example, if your elbow is hurting and feeling stiff, you may say, "Father, I know that by Jesus stripes my elbow has already been healed, therefore, I speak to my elbow (according to Matthew 17:20; 21:21; Mark 11:23) and I say pain leave my elbow right now in Jesus' Name! Elbow, I command you to bend and work normally and for all stiffness to get out of my elbow now!" That is one way

The Law of Faith

to make a withdrawal of healing (that is already yours) from your grace account. You release your faith the same way for finances. You might say, "Father, II Corinthians 8:9 says that Jesus was made poor for me on the cross. He bore all of my financial lack and poverty. He defeated it and redeemed me from it! He then gave me His financial prosperity in its place! Therefore, all financial lack and poverty I command you to get out of my home and finances right now in Jesus' Name! Money! Thousands of dollars, I command you to come into my accounts and finances!!"

Please let me insert this. The Bible says if you don't work you won't eat; so commanding financial blessings to be manifested in your life does not mean that you can sit around and do absolutely nothing. You still have to engage in some kind of work. Deuteronomy 8:18 says that God gives us the power or ability to get wealth. It did not say that God gives us wealth, but the ability to get it. The Lord also said that He will prosper whatever we set our hands to do. So, we need to be doing something. If you are being attacked with fear, then speak to it and command it to leave in Jesus' Name! I mentioned this before but it bears repeating. Deuteronomy 28:66 tells us that fear is a curse and Jesus has already redeemed us from the curse of the law (Galatians 3:13, 14).

In your grace account is freedom from fear, so release your faith and make a withdrawal. How do you do that again? Speak to fear and command it to get out of your life immediately in the Name of Jesus! God told the Apostle Paul that His grace was sufficient (more than enough) for him. I believe that when He said that to Paul He was reminding him that everything he needed was in His grace.

Grace, Faith, Rest

Also, since the grace of God was enough for Jesus to pay the penalty of sin for all of humanity then it is more than enough for you and me in every area of our lives!!

THE REST OF FAITH

Chapter 3

Praise the Lord! We have reached the 3rd level! Many of us have <u>tried</u> our best to operate on this level and have failed. I emphasized the word "tried" because that is where we have missed it so many times. We have tried our best to perform and to do all the "right" Christian things and many times it just seemed like we were spinning our wheels. We were taught that you have to do this and you have to do that, so we started doing all of these things but with the wrong motives and attitudes. I believe that a lot of those attitudes were attitudes of self-effort, almost trying to put on a spiritual performance for the Lord in hopes that He would see our great works and do something for us.

Do you remember what Jesus told the church at Ephesus in Revelation Chapter Two? He recognized all of their good works and labors, but He told them they had left their first love. The Lord wasn't against their good works. He made a point to emphasize the labor and works of all seven churches. He did not tell each church I know your heart, but He said I know your works. Once again, works for the Lord are very important, but they must be works of faith in Jesus that are born out of a heart of love; not works of self-effort. I believe that the church at Ephesus started off with works that came out of their deep and intimate fellowship with Jesus, but somewhere the devil deceived them in a very subtle way.

They continued on with their good works but it wasn't the result of maintaining their close walk with the Lord. Probably without realizing it they started thinking of more ways to do things for the Kingdom while spending less time getting to know the One who gave us the Kingdom. It seems that their goal became more about the works themselves. They became more works minded than knowing God minded. If we don't keep the right perspective on why we are serving the Lord, even our "religious" works can become an idol in our lives; coming between us and our relationship with God. The result probably caused them to step out from under grace into bondage back under the law. Why is this important? When you become more performance minded to the neglect of your intimate walk with the Lord, you will struggle more and more to experience His rest. You can't "work up" the rest of God. You can't earn it by being the most faithful worker in your church. God's rest is a supernatural rest. It can only be experienced through faith in the finished works of Christ! It is totally grace oriented! Let me share a few verses with you from Hebrews 3:18-4:3.

> "And to whom did He swear that they would not enter His rest, but to those who did not obey?
>
> So we see that they could not enter in because of unbelief.
>
> Therefore, since a promise remains of entering His rest, let us fear lest any of you seem to have come short of it.
>
> For indeed the gospel was preached to us as well as to them; but the word which they heard did not profit them, not being mixed with faith in those who heard it.
>
> For we who have believed do enter that rest, as He has said: "So I swore in My wrath, 'They shall not enter My rest,'" although the works were finished from the foundation of the world."

God said that the children of Israel could not enter into His rest because of their unbelief (which is disobedience and not believing God). If you believe God, you will believe His Word, and if you believe His Word you will obey it. So, it takes faith to experience God's supernatural rest. Therefore, getting back to these three levels, you should be able to see how being established in the first two levels is a prerequisite to operating on the third level. Many Christians want to experience God's supernatural rest but they do not have a revelation of grace or how to set the law of faith into motion. As the Bible said they came short of the rest of God. I don't want to come short do you? He said in verse 3 of chapter 4, **"...We who have <u>believed</u> do enter that rest..."** He did not say, "We who have doubled up on our praying and studying or we who have increased our church attendance or we who have increased how many times we go out witnessing do enter into rest..." did he?

God said that we have to <u>believe</u> to enter into His rest. So, the question should be, "What do we need to believe?" We must believe and have total confidence that Jesus finished everything for us at Calvary! I don't mean that we can just quote a few verses we learned a year ago about our redemption! I mean that we have made the time (and it is well worth our time) and spent hours upon hours studying and meditating on all that our Lord suffered for us to obtain our eternal redemption. We must believe with all of our hearts that we are already righteous, healed, delivered, and prosperous in Christ! We must believe that we already conquered the devil and we already have the victory in every area of our lives! All these things are already true and done for you and me in Christ Jesus! The more we know this, and I mean really know it, the more we will experience God's supernatural rest and peace in our daily lives!

I think we should go back to the example about the checking account. This is a very simple way to understand what God means about entering into rest because of your faith in what is already done. Let's say that I have $1000.00 in my checking account. Of course I would not have any doubts about it because I put it in there. I know it is in there. You could say that it is already finished for me. Well, God who cannot lie tells us in His Word everything He has already finished or deposited for us in our grace account.

Now, if I get a bill in the mail tomorrow for $150.00 I am not going to let it disturb me because I know, you could say, what is finished or done in my account. Are you following me? What if I don't have even one dollar in my

The Law of Faith

wallet when I get this bill, should I be bothered or worried about how I am going to pay it? Of course not! Why would I not have any stress or fears about paying this bill for $150.00? Because of the simple fact that I have $1000.00 in my account. Let me say it this way. I believe in what is already done for me in my checking account. So, even though I don't see the money yet, I am not worried about it at all. Can you see that I would actually be at rest about it even though (in the natural realm) I haven't paid it yet and do not have any money in my wallet? I would not have any fear about paying that bill and my heart would not be troubled. By the way, stress is the result of yielding to pressure. The devil cannot put us under any pressure concerning any area of our lives when we really know what is ours in Christ and how to appropriate it! The Lord Jesus has done everything for us so we can live in rest all of the time!

If I knew that I would always have more than enough money in my account to cover every bill that comes up, I would never experience stress from financial pressure again. Knowing that the money issue for me is finished would completely eliminate any financial pressure in my life. I would never view any bills from that point on as financial pressure, even if I don't have any money in my wallet at the time. Why would I have such rest and peace about my finances? It would be because of what I <u>believe</u> wouldn't it? I believe there is enough money in my account to cover any bill that may come up. I hope you can see where I am going with this. I didn't say this was real deep teaching. It is very simple teaching, but still very important revelation. Do you see where the supernatural rest comes from? It comes from believing and knowing what is already finished. In this example I was talking about the financial area of life, but it works the same in every area of life.

If you really believe that by Jesus' stripes you have already been healed, then you would know that healing and health is already finished for you and is already in your grace account. If you get up one morning and don't feel good or go to the doctor and he gives you a bad report, you should not experience any stress or worry, but supernatural rest and peace. Why? Because you know that even though you may not look or feel healed, your healing is still a done deal! You believe and know that in Christ you have plenty of healing in your spiritual account and it is time to make a withdrawal. Isaiah 53:3-5; Matthew 8:17 & I Peter 2:24 says it is in there and you believe it! You also know that you don't have to go on a quick fast, start doing more for your church and double up on your Bible reading to experience the healing that is already in your account. Release your faith, access God's grace and expect your healing to come to pass. Speak to your body and declare that it is healed, strong and healthy in Jesus' Name!

Remember, you have a right (you are God's righteousness in Christ-you now have rights in God's Kingdom) to withdraw every good thing God has provided for you through Jesus' sacrifice, conquest and resurrection! It is time we learn how to allow God's grace to reign in our lives. Entering into God's rest is the same as allowing God's grace to reign in our lives. Romans 5:20, 21 say:

The Law of Faith

"Moreover the law entered that the offense might abound. But where sin abounded, grace abounded much more,

So that as sin reigned in death, even so grace might reign through righteousness to eternal life through Jesus Christ our Lord."

Because of Adam's sin, the door was opened for sickness, disease, poverty and death to enter the world. According to verse 21, whenever you see a lost person, you are seeing sin reigning in their lives. A person who is lost is spiritually dead or has spiritual death in his spirit, therefore this spiritual death (separation from God) within him is a demonstration of sin reigning in his life. Really, if you think about it, since sickness, poverty and the curse are the result of sin entering the world, then sickness, poverty and anything under the curse of the law are a demonstration of sin reigning in a person's life.

The last half of verse 21 is the good news though, where it said that grace might reign through righteousness to eternal life. When you see a Christian, a person with eternal life, then you are seeing God's grace reigning aren't you? If sin can reign, grace can reign even more! Verse 20 said: **"...Where sin abounded, grace abounded much more."** Jesus obtained eternal redemption for us which includes spiritual life, forgiveness, health, prosperity and all the blessings of Heaven. When any of these things are being manifested in our lives then you are seeing and experiencing grace reigning! We cannot see grace with our natural eyes, but we can see the effect of it reigning in our lives. Let me remind you of a couple more Scriptures that describe grace reigning.

Grace, Faith, Rest

"And with great power the apostles gave witness to the resurrection of the Lord Jesus. And great grace was upon them all."
(Acts 4:33)

"And the hand of the Lord was with them, and a great number believed and turned to the Lord.
Then news of these things came to the ears of the church in Jerusalem, and they sent our Barnabas to go as far as Antioch.
When he came and had seen the grace of God, he was glad, and encouraged them all that with purpose of heart they should continue with the Lord." (Acts 11:21-23)

"And when James, Cephas, and John, who seemed to be pillars, perceived the grace that had been given to me..." (Galatians 2:9)

When God works salvations, healings, signs and wonders through Believers, you are seeing God's grace reigning. When you lead someone to the Lord that is grace reigning! When you receive your healing or a financial miracle that is grace reigning! So let grace reign in your life every day!! Now, if we don't allow God's grace to reign then we are frustrating it. Look with me at what the Apostle Paul said.

"We then, as workers together with Him also plead with you not to receive the grace of God in vain.
For He says: "In an acceptable time I have heard you, and in the day of salvation I have helped you."

Behold, now is the accepted time; behold, now is the day of salvation." (II Corinthians 6:1, 2)

He said that now is the day of salvation. Remember, salvation includes forgiveness, eternal life, peace, healing, prosperity and protection. Right now we have a right in Christ to experience all of these blessings, and if we don't then we are receiving God's grace in vain; in other words, we are not allowing the grace of God to rule and reign in our lives. For many Christians, God's grace reigns in their spirits through eternal life, but is not reigning in their bodies through perfect health, etc. We should expect to experience the grace of God reigning in every area of our lives in Jesus' Name!!

"I do not set aside the grace of God; for if righteousness comes through the law, then Christ died in vain." (Galatians 2:21)

In the New King James Bible, it says, "I do not set aside the grace of God..." In the King James Bible, it says, "I do not frustrate the grace of God..." To frustrate and set aside God's grace means not to believe and accept what Jesus finished and blessed us with through His grace at Calvary. If you refuse to believe that by Jesus' stripes you were healed, then you are setting aside God's grace in regards to healing for your body. You will actually be forfeiting the supernatural rest of God in your body.

In the case of healing, remember that disease is simply dis-ease. If your body is suffering with a disease then your body is not experiencing ease or rest, but when you receive your healing then your body has once again

Grace, Faith, Rest

entered into rest, then your healing is a demonstration of God's grace reigning in your body. If you will not take time to learn about all that Jesus did for you (for every area of your life) in His sufferings, death and resurrection, then those will be the areas where you will frustrate the grace of God and not enter (meaning experience the manifestation) into supernatural rest. Galatians 2:21 in the Living Bible says:

"I am not one of those who treats Christ's death as meaningless. For if we could be saved by keeping Jewish laws, then there was no need for Christ to die."

The Amplified Bible says: **"[Therefore, I do not treat God's gracious gift as something of minor importance and defeat its very purpose]; I do not set aside and invalidate and frustrate and nullify the grace (unmerited favor) of God..."**

I hope that you can see by what I just shared with you that you cannot enter into rest without allowing God's grace to reign in your life, and the grace of God will not reign in your life without setting the law of faith into motion. Remember, faith accesses God's grace (Romans 5:2). One more thing, if your faith is in your performance; instead of Jesus and His finished works then you have not set the law of faith into operation; which means that you have not energized and activated your faith to work for you. You could say that you are trying to get something out of the bank without making a withdrawal. You could also say that you are frustrating or setting aside your bank account. The money is there but you are not getting any of it out. God's grace has been there for us all this time. Why don't we start making some withdrawals? Once again, we must keep our faith grounded and established in Jesus and His finished works and then put forth every effort to release our faith and receive from God, what He has already done for us! Hebrews 4:9-11 say:

"There remains therefore a rest for the people of God.
For he who has entered His rest has himself also ceased from his works as God did from His.
Let us therefore be diligent to enter that rest, lest anyone fall according to the same example of disobedience."

In verse 9 the Lord said that if you have entered His rest you have ceased from your works, then He said in verse 11 to be diligent to enter that rest. In the King James Bible, it says, **"Let us labour therefore to enter into that rest..."** If you look up the word "labor" in the Greek, it means to use speed, to make effort, be prompt and be diligent. Now, if you did not understand the difference between works of faith and works of self-effort then you might think that He was contradicting Himself in those two verses, but He wasn't. God's Word translation says it this way:

"So we must make every effort to enter that place of rest. Then no one will be lost by following the example of those who refused to obey."

In Hebrews 4:10 where God said that if we have entered His rest then we have ceased from our works, He is simply reminding us that faith accesses God's grace and we have to believe to enter into the rest of God, or you could say that we must put the law of faith into operation to enter God's rest. The way to put the law of faith into operation is through works of faith, not works of self-effort. So, in Hebrews 4:11 when He talks about laboring to enter into rest, that laboring is referring to works of faith; works that come forth from a heart that believes in the finished works of Christ. The Lord Jesus described the main way we are to release our faith or the main way to put works with our faith when He told us to <u>speak</u> to the mountain in Mark 11:23. He told us to speak and declare what we <u>believe</u> in our hearts will come to pass. From that point on we are to rejoice, praise the Lord and act like it's done!

For example, the way to labor to enter into rest concerning your healing would be to call yourself healed and to praise God for it while you don't feel or look healed. You know as well as I do that if your body is really hurting, you don't feel like declaring you are healed. You don't feel like praising God that He has already healed you, do you? It is definitely a labor to do that! It's easy to release your faith for other people because you are not physically experiencing their pain and suffering, but if your body feels miserable and just wants to complain and go to bed, then you have to make yourself put for an effort to release your faith because your flesh does not feel like confesses the Word and praising God! That is what the Bible means by being diligent to enter into that rest.

Therefore, it is definitely a labor to put forth a genuine effort to command the pain to leave your body and to begin rejoicing because you believe it's done! Those kind of

The Law of Faith

works are called works of faith and when you labor to show forth those kind of works you will access God's grace and start experiencing His rest! Mark 4:35-41 is one of my favorite stories in the Bible where Jesus gave us an awesome example of how to enter into rest despite horrible circumstances around you. This story is a great illustration of how to use our faith, and it is something that we should take time to meditate on and read over and over again!

"On the same day, when evening had come, He said to them, "Let us cross over to the other side."

Now when they had left the multitude, they took Him along in the boat as He was. And other little boats were also with Him.

And a great windstorm arose, and the waves beat into the boat, so that it was already filling.

But He was in the stern, asleep on a pillow. And they awoke Him and said to Him, "Teacher, do You not care that we are perishing?"

Then He arose and rebuked the wind, and said to the sea, "Peace, be still!" And the wind ceased and there was a great calm.

But He said to them, "Why are you so fearful? How is it that you have no faith?"

And they feared exceedingly, and said to one another, "Who can this be, that even the wind and the sea obey Him!"

According to what we just read, before Jesus and His disciples set sail, He specifically released His faith. As it is written in Mark 11:23 and II Corinthians 4:13, He set the law of faith into motion. You may ask, "How do you know He did?" Because of what He said before they set sail. He said, "Let us cross over to the other side." He believed in His heart that what He said out of His mouth would come to pass or would happen in the natural realm. You may be thinking right now that you already know what I am teaching, and since you have studied a lot about how to release your faith, you don't need to hear this anymore, but it is still very good to hear it again. I never get tired of hearing the Word over and over again because I know that my faith will just keep on increasing and will grow stronger and stronger. It's not that I am getting more faith, but I am learning how to more effectively use the measure of faith I already have. (We have 2 other books on faith that would be very helpful to you). "How to Respond to a bad Report" and "Just Believe".

I especially like the part where the Bible says that Jesus took a nap. He was actually in the stern and fell asleep on a pillow, but that was after He said they would cross over to the other side; obviously, to you and me, that means He entered into rest, wouldn't you agree? Once again, when did He take a nap? Was it before He set the law of faith into motion or after? It was afterwards; that is, after He spoke the command of faith. Now, when did the devil start the storm? Was it before Jesus released His faith or after? It was after Jesus <u>spoke</u> and put the law of faith into operation. Remember, the law of faith is called a law because it always works. As I said in chapter two, the law of gravity always works unless a higher law is introduced to override it, but if a higher law is not introduced then no one can just decide to stop the law of gravity from working. That means you can count on the law of gravity to work, you don't have to wonder if it is going to work this time.

The Law of Faith

Entering into God's rest is believing that Jesus finished everything for us at Calvary, but there is also a rest that you enter into by knowing that once God's spiritual laws (I am not talking about Jewish Laws, but the laws and forces that govern God's Kingdom) and forces are set in motion there is not any man or demon who can stop them from working for you! Also, God's spiritual laws and forces are not activated through positive thinking. Positive thinking is very important because we must renew our minds to God's Word so we will know what to say; but we still must speak the Word of God! Just thinking that you are healed does not release any faith. Sometimes you will hear people say, "Our thoughts are with the family who lost a loved one or our thoughts are with you in this unfortunate situation."

I know they are trying to say something nice to those who are going through a rough time in their lives, but still, what they said has no faith or power to do anything to help them! Faith is not released through our thoughts; it's released through our words! We must say something! Words can be used as faith containers. If you want to help the family or an individual person then pray (you speak words when you pray) for them, release your faith and believe God to manifest His peace and strength in their lives, and also pray that they will experience God's Presence in their lives and His great love for them. Something else that would be important to pray is for God to send Christian laborers to them (and you may be one of those laborers) that will share the Gospel with them, bring them food and anything else they may need. When you pray, you are releasing your faith through words so God's grace and power can be demonstrated in their lives.

Grace, Faith, Rest

Our Heavenly Father gave us the example we are to follow where releasing our faith is concerned. In Hebrews 11:3 the Bible says that through faith God created the worlds in the beginning. Hebrews 1:3 says that God upholds all things by the <u>word</u> of His power. It did not say He upholds all things by the thoughts of His power. In Genesis chapter one, the phrase "And God said" is used at least eight times when He brought all of creation into existence. It did not say, "And God thought let there be light, etc." God is the one who gave us the law of faith and He is also the one who told us how to set it into motion so we can access His grace. We don't get to make up our own way to activate God's spiritual laws and forces, we have to do it God's way, but we need to remember that because faith is a law, it will always work for us when we learn how to use and release our faith.

Back to our story about Jesus in the middle of a storm, I wanted you to see that the storm did not start until Jesus set the law of faith in motion and it did not stop until they arrived at the other side. Before Jesus released His faith and after the miracle came to pass there was no storm. Many times the devil will wait until you pray the prayer of faith or speak the command of faith to start the storm, like he did against Jesus, and this is where our rest should come in. We need to recognize the devil's deceptive tactics. The Lord made it very clear to His disciples that they were not in faith didn't He? You can tell when you read this account that the disciples were afraid, worried and scared. These words are not synonymous for entering into God's supernatural rest.

The Law of Faith

The devil succeeded with his ploy where the disciples were concerned, but not where Jesus was concerned. Because Jesus really believed that the law of faith would work, He took a nap didn't He? The devil wants you and me to think that he can stop the law of faith from working, but we know that he can't! It is impossible for the devil to stop your faith from working after you have truly released it! Our enemy knows that, but he hopes that you don't know that. His strategy is to manipulate circumstances and situations to deceive you into believing and confessing that your faith isn't working. He cannot shut your faith down, only you can! So, his goal is to see if he can convince you to shut down the law of faith which you set into motion. Since he cannot stop that spiritual law from working for you, then no matter what he says or does, recognize it's a lie, and stand tall and strong on the Word of God holding fast to your confession of faith without wavering because your faith (or confidence) has great reward!!

"Therefore do not cast away your confidence, which has great reward.
For you have need of endurance, so that after you have done the will of God, you may receive the promise:" (Hebrews 10:35, 36)

I want to say one more time as we come to the end of this book, we need to be so confident and established in all that Jesus finished for us through His substitutionary sacrifice that we know the devil cannot rewrite it or change it in any way! We know that we know that everything is already done for us in Christ, and as we release our faith (as the Bible teaches) God's grace will be accessed and we will start experiencing and enjoying the exceeding riches

Grace, Faith, Rest

of the glory of our inheritance in the Lord! We will live our lives every day in perfect peace and in the supernatural rest of God! No matter what storms my come we will stay at rest in faith and grace, and not be moved by anything our enemy brings against us! We will always put works with our faith, not to pressure God to respond to us, but to respond to every good thing He has already done for us! His grace is more than enough for us (Ephesians 1:7) and Jesus is our all sufficiency in all things!! I praise God and give Him all the glory for His grace, faith and rest!

About the Author

Dwayne Norman is a 1978 graduate of Christ for The Nations Bible Institute in Dallas, Texas. He spent 3 years witnessing to prostitutes and pimps in the red light district of Dallas, and another 3 years ministering as a team leader in the Campus Challenge ministry of Dr. Norvel Hayes. He was ordained by Pastor Buddy and Pat Harrison of Faith Christian Fellowship in Tulsa, Oklahoma in September 1980. He also taught evangelism classes several times at Dr. Hayes' Bible school in Tennessee.

Soon the Lord led him to go on the road ministering. He ministers powerfully on soul winning, and on how God wants to use all Believers in demonstrating His Kingdom not just in Word but also in Power!

He teaches with clarity, the work that God accomplished for all believers in Christ from the cross to the throne, and the importance of this revelation to the church for the fulfillment of Jesus' commission to make disciples of all nations.

He strongly believes that we are called to do the works Jesus did and greater works in His Name, not just in church but especially in the marketplace.

He and his wife Leia travel and teach Supernatural Evangelism and train Believers in who they are in Christ and how to operate in their ministries. He teaches the

Word on internet radio Monday through Friday at 4PM Eastern Standard time on wofr.org (The Word of Faith Radio Network). His program is called Victory in the Word.

He has also downloaded at least 150 audio messages to youtube.com that you can listen to. As of the writing of this book, he has written 17 teaching books which are available on their ministry website:
www.dwaynenormanministries.org

His books are also available on amazon.com as Kindle books.

To inquire for meetings with Dwayne and Leia Norman, please contact them at:

Dwayne & Leia Norman
124 Evergreen Court
Mount Sterling, Kentucky   40353

(859) 351-6496
dwayne7@att.net
website: www.dwaynenormanministries.org

Made in the USA
Lexington, KY
26 August 2017